From Dream to Done

DILBAGH SINGH

Published by DILBAGH SINGH, 2023.

FROM DREAM TO DONE

First edition. May 14, 2023.

Copyright © 2023 DILBAGH SINGH.

ISBN: 979-8223331650

Written by DILBAGH SINGH.

Table of Contents

Introduction

We all have dreams and aspirations in life, but achieving them can often feel overwhelming and out of reach. Whether it's starting a business, pursuing a new career, or simply improving our health and well-being, it's easy to get stuck in the dreaming phase and struggle to take action.

That's where this book comes in. From Dream to Done: Strategies for Achieving Your Life Goals is a practical guide to help you turn your dreams into reality. Through a series of chapters focused on specific topics, this book will provide you with actionable strategies and tips to help you stay motivated, focused, and on track towards achieving your goals.

Drawing on real-life examples and expert insights, this book will explore a range of topics including time management, building positive habits, managing stress, adapting to change, and maintaining momentum. Each chapter will provide practical advice and exercises to help you apply these strategies to your own life, as well as case studies of individuals who have successfully achieved their goals using these methods.

Whether you're just starting out on your journey towards your life goals, or you're feeling stuck and in need of inspiration, From Dream to Done will provide you with the tools and motivation you need to make your dreams a reality. So let's get started!

About Author

Dilbagh Singh, a passionate individual from Delhi, India, who believes that everyone has the potential to turn their dreams into reality. Dilbagh is a graduate of Delhi University and has spent years researching and exploring different strategies to help individuals achieve their life goals. With his book, "From Dream to Done: Strategies for Achieving Your Life Goals," Dilbagh shares his knowledge and expertise to help readers overcome obstacles, stay motivated, and reach their full potential. This book is a culmination of Dilbagh's years of experience and is a must-read for anyone looking to turn their dreams into reality.

"All our dreams[1] can come true if we have the courage[2] to pursue them."

- Walt Disney

---

1. *https://www.invajy.com/dreams-quotes/*

2. *https://www.invajy.com/41-courage-quotes-to-enhance-your-inner-strength/*

1. Defining Your Life Goals:

Identifying and Clarifying
What You Really Want

(In this chapter, you'll learn how to define your life goals and why it's important to be specific and clear about what you want to achieve)

Introduction:

Many people spend their lives feeling unfulfilled or unsatisfied because they don't have clear goals to work towards. Defining your life goals is the first step towards living a purpose-driven life and achieving your dreams. In this chapter, we'll explore why it's important to identify and clarify your life goals, and provide practical tools and strategies for doing so.

Why Define Your Life Goals?

Defining your life goals is important for several reasons:

1. Gives You Clarity: When you have clear goals, you know what you're working towards and why. This clarity can help you stay motivated and focused.

1. Increases Motivation: When you have something to work towards, you're more motivated to take action and make progress towards your goals.

1. Helps Prioritize: With clear goals, you can prioritize your time and energy, focusing on what's most important and valuable to you.

1. Guides Decision-Making: Your goals can help guide your decision-making, making it easier to say "yes" or "no" to opportunities that align with your vision.

1. Provides Direction: When you have clear goals, you have direction in life, and you're less likely to feel lost or directionless.

How to Define Your Life Goals:

1. Get Clear on Your Values: Your values are the guiding principles that shape your life. Spend some time reflecting on what matters most to you and why. What are your top values? How do they align with your life goals?

Story Example:

Meet Daisy, a successful corporate lawyer in her late 30s. Despite her professional achievements, Daisy felt unfulfilled and unhappy in her personal life. She realized that she had been chasing success and validation from others, without taking the time to reflect on what she truly wanted. Daisy decided to take a break from her demanding job and embark on a journey of self-discovery. She spent several weeks journaling and meditating on her values, and realized that she had been neglecting her creativity and passion for writing. She also realized that her top values were freedom, creativity, and authenticity.

1. Brainstorm Your Dreams: Take some time to dream big and brainstorm all the things you'd like to accomplish in your life. Don't worry about whether they're realistic or not, just let your imagination run wild.

Story Example:

Daisy took some time to think about her dreams and realized that she had always wanted to write a novel. She had never pursued it because she felt that it wasn't a practical or financially secure career choice. But during her break, Daisy allowed herself to dream big and visualize what her life would look like if she pursued her passion for writing. She imagined herself as a successful author, living a life of freedom and creativity.

1. Prioritize Your Goals: Once you've brainstormed your dreams, prioritize them based on what's most important to you. What goals align with your values? What goals would bring you the most joy and fulfillment?

Story Example:

Daisy realized that writing a novel aligned with her top values of freedom, creativity, and authenticity. She decided to make writing her top priority and committed to making progress on her novel every day, even if it was just for a few minutes.

1. Make Your Goals SMART: SMART stands for Specific, Measurable, Achievable, Relevant, and Time-bound. Make sure your goals meet these criteria, so you have a clear roadmap for achieving them.

STORY EXAMPLE:

Daisy set a SMART goal to finish writing her novel within a year. She broke down the goal into smaller, achievable steps and worked on same.

Conclusion

Defining your life goals is a crucial step towards achieving success and fulfillment. By identifying your values, passions, and setting SMART goals, you can create a clear roadmap for your future and take control of your life. Remember to be patient and persistent, as achieving your goals may take time and effort, but the rewards are well worth it.

2. Understanding Your Motivation:

Finding Your Inner Drive to Succeed

(This chapter explores the different types of motivation and how to tap into your own inner drive to help you stay focused on your life goals.)

Introduction:

Motivation is what drives us to achieve our goals and succeed in life. However, motivation is not one-size-fits-all. Everyone is motivated differently, and understanding your own motivation can help you tap into your inner drive to succeed. In this chapter, we'll explore the different types of motivation and provide strategies for understanding your own motivation to help you stay focused on your life goals.

Types of Motivation:

There are two main types of motivation: intrinsic and extrinsic.

1. Intrinsic Motivation: Intrinsic motivation comes from within. It's the drive to achieve something because it's personally meaningful or enjoyable. People who are intrinsically motivated are more likely to stick with a task or goal, even if it's challenging.

1. Extrinsic Motivation: Extrinsic motivation comes from external factors, such as rewards, recognition, or social pressure. While extrinsic motivation can be effective in the short-term, it's often less sustainable than intrinsic motivation.

Understanding Your Motivation:

Understanding your own motivation is key to achieving your goals. Here are some strategies to help you tap into your inner drive to succeed:

1. Reflect on Your Why: Reflect on why you want to achieve your goals. What's driving you to succeed? What's the deeper purpose or meaning behind your goal?

Story Example:

Daisy reflected on why she wanted to write a novel. She realized that she had always loved storytelling and wanted to share her passion with others. She also wanted to prove to herself that she could accomplish something challenging.

1. Identify Your Values: Identify your personal values and how they relate to your goals. When your goals align with your values, you'll be more motivated to achieve them.

Story Example:

Daisy identified her values of creativity and self-expression , which aligned with her goal of writing a novel.

1. Set Meaningful Goals: Set goals that are personally meaningful and aligned with your values. When your goals are meaningful to you, you'll be more motivated to achieve them.

Story Example:

Daisy set a meaningful goal of writing a novel within a year, which aligned with her values of creativity and self-expression.

1. Find Inspiration: Surround yourself with inspiration. Seek out role models, read books or articles related to your goal, and visualize yourself achieving your goal.

Story Example:

Daisy found inspiration by reading novels by her favorite authors and attending writing workshops. She also visualized herself holding a published copy of her own novel.

1. Practice Self-Care: Take care of yourself physically, emotionally, and mentally. When you feel good, you'll be more motivated to take action towards your goals.

Story Example:

Daisy practiced self-care by taking breaks when she needed to, eating healthy meals, and practicing mindfulness meditation to manage her stress levels.

Conclusion:

Understanding your motivation is key to achieving your life goals. By tapping into your inner drive to succeed, you can stay focused, motivated, and on track towards achieving your dreams. Remember to reflect on your why, identify your values, set meaningful goals, find inspiration, and practice self-care to stay motivated and achieve your goals.

3. Setting SMART Goals:

How to Set Goals that Are Specific, Measurable, Achievable, Relevant, and Time-bound

(Here, you'll learn a proven framework for setting effective goals that are aligned with your vision and values.)

Introduction:

Setting goals is a critical step in achieving success. However, not all goals are created equal. Setting SMART goals ensures that your goals are specific, measurable, achievable, relevant, and time-bound. In this chapter, we'll explore the benefits of setting SMART goals and provide a framework for setting effective goals that are aligned with your vision and values.

Benefits of Setting SMART Goals:

Setting SMART goals has several benefits:

1. Clarity: SMART goals provide clarity on what you want to achieve and how you'll achieve it.

1. Motivation: SMART goals are more motivating because they're specific and meaningful.

1. Focus: SMART goals help you focus your efforts and resources towards achieving your objectives.

1. Accountability: SMART goals provide a clear way to measure progress and hold yourself accountable.

The SMART Framework:

The SMART framework is a proven way to set effective goals. Here's what each letter stands for:

1. Specific: Your goal should be specific and clearly defined. Avoid vague goals that are difficult to measure or achieve.

1. Measurable: Your goal should be measurable so that you can track progress and know when you've achieved it.

1. Achievable: Your goal should be challenging but achievable. Set goals that stretch you but are still within reach.

1. Relevant: Your goal should be relevant to your vision, values, and long-term objectives.

1. Time-bound: Your goal should have a specific deadline or timeframe. This creates a sense of urgency and helps you stay focused on achieving your goal.

How to Set SMART Goals:

1. Define Your Vision: Start by defining your long-term vision for your life. What do you want to achieve? Where do you want to be in five or ten years?

Story Example:
Daisy defined her long-term vision of becoming a published author and earning a living from writing.

1. Identify Your Values: Identify your personal values and how

they relate to your vision. Your goals should align with your values to provide a sense of purpose and meaning.

Story Example:

Daisy identified her values of creativity and self-expression, which aligned with her long-term vision of becoming a published author.

1. Set Specific Goals: Set specific goals that are aligned with your vision and values. Your goals should be clear, concise, and measurable.

Story Example:

Daisy set a specific goal of writing a novel within a year and self-publishing it.

1. Make Your Goals Achievable: Ensure that your goals are achievable but challenging. Break down larger goals into smaller, more manageable tasks to avoid feeling overwhelmed.

Story Example:

Daisy broke down her goal of writing a novel into smaller tasks, such as writing for one hour every day and outlining each chapter before writing.

1. Ensure Your Goals Are Relevant: Ensure that your goals are relevant to your long-term vision and values. Avoid setting goals that don't align with your vision or are not personally meaningful.

Story Example:

Daisy's goal of writing a novel aligned with her long-term vision of becoming a published author and expressing her creativity.

1. Set a Deadline: Set a specific deadline for achieving your goal.

This creates a sense of urgency and helps you stay focused on your objective.

Story Example:
Daisy set a deadline of one year to write and self-publish her novel.
Conclusion:
Setting SMART goals is a critical step in achieving success. By following the SMART framework, you can set effective goals that are specific, measurable, achievable, relevant, and time-bound. Remember to define your vision.

4. Creating a Roadmap to Success:

Mapping Out the Steps You Need to Take

(This chapter teaches you how to create a roadmap that breaks down your big goals into smaller, manageable steps to help you stay on track.)

Introduction:

Once you've set your goals, it's important to create a roadmap that breaks down your big goals into smaller, manageable steps. A roadmap helps you stay on track and provides a clear path towards achieving your objectives. In this chapter, we'll explore how to create a roadmap to success and provide strategies for staying motivated and focused.

Why Create a Roadmap:

Creating a roadmap has several benefits:

1. Clarity: A roadmap provides clarity on the steps you need to take to achieve your goals.

1. Focus: A roadmap helps you stay focused on your priorities and avoid getting distracted.

1. Motivation: A roadmap provides a sense of progress and helps you stay motivated towards achieving your goals.

1. Accountability: A roadmap provides a clear way to measure progress and hold yourself accountable.

The Roadmap Framework:

The roadmap framework is a simple way to break down your big goals into smaller, manageable steps. Here's what each step involves:

1. Define Your Goal: Start by defining your big goal. This should be a specific, measurable, achievable, relevant, and time-bound (SMART) goal.

Story Example:
Daisy's big goal was to write and self-publish a novel within a year.

1. Identify Milestones: Identify the key milestones that you need to achieve to reach your goal. These are major accomplishments that mark progress towards your goal.

Story Example:
Daisy's milestones included outlining each chapter, completing the first draft, editing and revising the manuscript, designing the book cover, and publishing the book.

1. Break It Down: Break down each milestone into smaller, manageable steps. These are the specific actions that you need to take to achieve each milestone.

STORY EXAMPLE:
To outline each chapter, Daisy broke it down into steps such as brainstorming ideas, outlining the main plot points, and fleshing out the details.

1. Set Deadlines: Set deadlines for each step and milestone. This creates a sense of urgency and helps you stay focused on your objectives.

Story Example:

Daisy set deadlines for each milestone and step, such as completing the first draft within six months and publishing the book within a year.

1. Track Progress: Track your progress towards each milestone and adjust your roadmap as necessary. This helps you stay on track and make adjustments as you encounter obstacles.

Story Example:

Daisy tracked her progress towards each milestone by keeping a writing journal and making notes on her progress each day. She adjusted her roadmap as necessary by making changes to her writing schedule or adjusting her deadlines.

Staying Motivated and Focused:

Creating a roadmap is just the first step towards achieving your goals. Here are some strategies for staying motivated and focused:

1. Celebrate Small Wins: Celebrate each milestone and step that you achieve. This provides a sense of progress and helps you stay motivated towards achieving your goals.

1. Stay Accountable: Share your roadmap with someone you trust and *ask* them to hold you accountable. This provides support and encouragement as you work towards your objectives.

1. Stay Focused: Avoid getting distracted by other priorities and stay focused on your roadmap. Prioritize your tasks and stay committed to achieving your goals.

Conclusion:

Creating a roadmap is a critical step towards achieving success. By following the roadmap framework, you can break down your big goals into smaller, manageable steps and stay on track towards achieving your objectives. Remember to track your progress, celebrate your wins, and stay accountable as you work towards your goals. With a roadmap in place, you can stay motivated and focused on achieving your dreams.

5. Overcoming Obstacles:

Strategies for Dealing with Challenges and Setbacks

(In this chapter, you'll learn how to anticipate and overcome common obstacles that can derail your progress, such as fear, self-doubt, and procrastination.)

Introduction:

When working towards your goals, it's inevitable that you'll encounter obstacles and setbacks along the way. These can include fear, self-doubt, procrastination, and unexpected challenges. However, with the right strategies, you can overcome these obstacles and stay focused on achieving your objectives. In this chapter, we'll explore how to anticipate and overcome common obstacles and provide strategies for dealing with setbacks.

Anticipating Obstacles:

The first step towards overcoming obstacles is to anticipate them. This means identifying potential challenges that you may face and preparing for them in advance. Here are some common obstacles that you may encounter:

1. Fear: Fear can be a powerful obstacle that prevents you from taking action towards your goals. This can include fear of failure, fear of success, or fear of the unknown.

1. Self-Doubt: Self-doubt can also be a major obstacle, causing you

to doubt your abilities and question whether you're capable of achieving your goals.

1. Procrastination: Procrastination can be a difficult obstacle to overcome, as it can prevent you from taking action towards your goals and lead to feelings of guilt and frustration.

1. Unexpected Challenges: There may be unexpected challenges that arise, such as illness, financial setbacks, or family emergencies.

Story Example:

Daisy encountered several obstacles when writing and self-publishing her novel. She experienced fear of failure, self-doubt about her writing abilities, and procrastination when faced with writer's block. Additionally, she experienced unexpected challenges, such as a family emergency that required her attention.

Strategies for Overcoming Obstacles:

Once you've identified potential obstacles, you can prepare for them in advance. Here are some strategies for overcoming common obstacles:

1. Address Fear Head-On: Identify the root cause of your fear and develop a plan to overcome it. This may involve seeking support from friends or family, breaking down your goals into smaller steps, or seeking professional help if necessary.

Story Example:

Daisy addressed her fear of failure by reminding herself that writing and publishing a book was a long-term goal that required consistent effort. She also broke down her goals into smaller steps, such as writing for a specific amount of time each day, to help her overcome her fear of the unknown.

1. Challenge Self-Doubt: When you experience self-doubt,

challenge the negative thoughts and beliefs that are holding you back. Remind yourself of your strengths and past accomplishments, and focus on taking action towards your goals.

Story Example:

Daisy challenged her self-doubt by reminding herself of her passion for writing and the positive feedback she received from her beta readers. She also focused on taking action towards her goals, such as setting aside time each day to write and reaching out to potential cover designers.

1. Break Tasks into Smaller Steps: When faced with procrastination, break tasks into smaller, manageable steps. This can help you build momentum and overcome feelings of overwhelm.

Story Example:

Daisy broke down her writing tasks into smaller steps, such as outlining each chapter and setting a specific word count goal for each writing session. This helped her overcome writer's block and stay focused on her writing.

1. Stay Flexible: When unexpected challenges arise, stay flexible and adapt your plans as necessary. This may involve adjusting your goals or timelines to accommodate unexpected circumstances.

Story Example:

When faced with a family emergency, Daisy adjusted her writing schedule and deadlines to allow her to focus on her family. She also sought support from her writing community and received encouragement and understanding.

Conclusion:

Overcoming obstacles is a crucial part of achieving your goals. By anticipating potential challenges and developing strategies for dealing with them, you can stay motivated and focused even in the face of adversity. Remember to be patient, persistent, and kind to yourself, and celebrate your successes along the way.

6. Staying Accountable:

How to Stay on Track and Hold Yourself Responsible

(Here, you'll discover strategies for staying accountable and holding yourself responsible for making progress towards your goals.)

Introduction:

Setting goals is one thing, but staying accountable and making progress towards them is another. Accountability is crucial for achieving success, but it's not always easy to stay on track. In this chapter, we'll explore strategies for staying accountable and holding yourself responsible for making progress towards your goals.

The Importance of Accountability:

Accountability is the act of being responsible for your actions and decisions. When it comes to achieving goals, accountability is crucial for several reasons:

Motivation: Accountability provides motivation to keep working towards your goals.

Progress: Being accountable helps you track your progress and stay focused on your objectives.

Commitment: Being accountable helps you stay committed to your goals and prevents you from giving up.

Self-awareness: Being accountable helps you identify areas for improvement and learn from your mistakes.

Strategies for Staying Accountable:

Here are some strategies for staying accountable and holding yourself responsible for making progress towards your goals:

1. Write Down Your Goals:

Writing down your goals makes them more tangible and helps you stay focused on achieving them. Make sure to include specific details, such as deadlines and action steps, to make your goals more actionable.

Story Example:

Daisy wrote down her goal of writing a novel within a year and self-publishing it. She included specific action steps, such as writing for one hour every day and outlining each chapter before writing.

2. Find an Accountability Partner:

An accountability partner is someone who can hold you responsible for making progress towards your goals. This can be a friend, family member, or mentor who is supportive of your goals and willing to help keep you on track.

Story Example:

Daisy found an accountability partner in her writing group. They checked in with each other regularly and provided feedback on each other's work.

3. Use Technology:

There are many technological tools available to help you stay accountable, such as goal-tracking apps or habit-forming apps. These tools can help you track your progress and provide reminders to stay on track.

Story Example:

Daisy used a goal-tracking app to keep track of her daily writing progress and remind herself of her deadlines.

4. Set Milestones:

Breaking down larger goals into smaller milestones can make them more manageable and help you track your progress more easily. Celebrate each milestone as you reach it to keep yourself motivated.

Story Example:
Daisy set milestones for each chapter of her novel and celebrated each one by treating herself to a special reward.

5. Review Your Progress:

Regularly reviewing your progress towards your goals can help you identify areas for improvement and make any necessary adjustments. Use this review process as an opportunity to learn from your mistakes and celebrate your successes.

Story Example:
Daisy reviewed her progress towards her goal of writing a novel every week and adjusted her writing schedule to better fit her lifestyle.

Conclusion:
Staying accountable and holding yourself responsible for making progress towards your goals is crucial for achieving success. By writing down your goals, finding an accountability partner, using technology, setting milestones, and regularly reviewing your progress, you can stay on track and achieve your objectives. Remember to stay committed to your goals and celebrate each milestone along the way

7. Time Management:

Making the Most of Your Time and Energy

(This chapter teaches you how to manage your time and energy effectively, so you can focus on the things that matter most to you.)

Introduction:
Time management is a critical skill for achieving success. Effective time management allows you to make the most of your time and energy, so you can focus on the things that matter most to you. In this chapter, we'll explore the benefits of time management and provide strategies for managing your time and energy effectively.

Benefits of Time Management:

Time management has several benefits:

Increased productivity: Time management helps you use your time more efficiently, which increases your productivity.

Reduced stress: Effective time management helps you avoid procrastination and reduces the stress associated with missed deadlines and unfinished tasks.

Improved decision-making: Time management allows you to allocate time for decision-making and ensures that you have enough time to make thoughtful, well-informed decisions.

Better work-life balance: Effective time management ensures that you have enough time to devote to both your personal and professional life.

Strategies for Managing Your Time and Energy:

1. Set Priorities: Start by identifying your top priorities. What are

the most important things you need to do? Focus on the tasks that will have the biggest impact on your goals and vision.

Story Example:

Daisy identified her top priorities, which included writing her novel, spending time with her family, and taking care of her health.

1. Create a Schedule: Create a schedule that includes your top priorities and allocate time for each task. Use a planner or a calendar app to keep track of your schedule.

Story Example:

Daisy created a schedule that included time for writing, exercise, and spending time with her family.

1. Use Time-Blocking: Use time-blocking to manage your time more effectively. Time-blocking involves dividing your day into blocks of time and allocating specific tasks to each block.

Story Example:

Daisy used time-blocking to allocate specific times for writing, exercise, and spending time with her family.

1. Eliminate Distractions: Eliminate distractions that can derail your productivity, such as social media notifications, email alerts, and phone calls. Turn off notifications and set aside specific times to check your email and social media accounts.

Story Example:

Daisy turned off notifications on her phone and computer while writing and only checked her email and social media accounts during designated times.

1. Take Breaks: Take regular breaks to recharge your energy and improve your focus. Take a short walk, meditate, or do some stretching exercises.

Story Example:

Daisy took a short break every hour to stretch and do some deep breathing exercises.

1. Evaluate Your Progress: Evaluate your progress regularly to ensure that you're staying on track and making progress towards your goals. Make adjustments to your schedule and strategies as needed.

Story Example:

Daisy evaluated her progress weekly to ensure that she was making progress towards her goal of writing her novel. She made adjustments to her schedule and strategies as needed.

Conclusion:

Effective time management is essential for achieving success. By setting priorities, creating a schedule, using time-blocking, eliminating distractions, taking breaks, and evaluating your progress, you can manage your time and energy effectively and focus on the things that matter most to you. Remember, time is a valuable resource, so use it wisely

8. Building Habits for Success:

How to Develop Positive Habits That Support Your Goals

(In this chapter, you'll learn how to build positive habits that support your goals, such as daily exercise, meditation, or journaling.)

Introduction:

Success is not achieved overnight, it is the result of consistent and deliberate efforts towards our goals. Building positive habits is a critical step in achieving long-term success. In this chapter, we'll explore the importance of habits and provide a framework for developing positive habits that support your goals.

Why Habits Matter:

Habits are the small actions we take every day that add up to create our daily routines and ultimately shape our lives. Positive habits help us stay focused, energized, and motivated, while negative habits can hold us back and make it harder to achieve our goals.

The Habits Framework:

The habits framework is a proven way to develop positive habits. Here are the steps:

1. Define Your Goals: Start by defining your goals and the habits you need to develop to achieve them.

Story Example:

Daisy defined her goal of becoming a published author and identified the habits she needed to develop, such as writing every day and reading more.

1. Start Small: Focus on developing one habit at a time. Starting small makes it easier to stick with the habit and build momentum over time.

Story Example:

Daisy started by committing to write for 30 minutes every day, gradually increasing the time as she got used to the habit.

1. Set a Cue: A cue is a trigger that prompts you to perform the habit. This could be a specific time of day, a location, or an action that precedes the habit.

Story Example:

Daisy set a cue for her writing habit by committing to write every day at the same time and in the same location.

1. Develop a Routine: Once you have a cue, develop a routine that helps you perform the habit consistently. This could be a specific sequence of actions that you follow every time you perform the habit.

Story Example:

Daisy developed a routine for her writing habit that included making a cup of tea, setting up her writing space, and reviewing her outline before starting to write.

1. Reward Yourself: Rewards help reinforce the habit and make it more enjoyable. Choose a reward that aligns with your values and motivates you to stick with the habit.

Story Example:

Daisy rewarded herself with a favorite snack or a chapter of a book she was reading after completing her daily writing goal.

1. Review and Adjust: Regularly review your progress and adjust your habits as needed. Be honest with yourself and make changes that help you achieve your goals more effectively.

Story Example:

Daisy reviewed her progress weekly and adjusted her writing routine when she found that she was not making enough progress, such as waking up earlier to have more time to write.

Conclusion:

Developing positive habits is essential for achieving long-term success. By following the habits framework, you can develop positive habits that support your goals and help you achieve success. Remember to start small, set a cue, develop a routine, reward yourself, and regularly review and adjust your habits.

9. Building a Support Network:

Finding and Cultivating Relationships that Help You Succeed

(Here, you'll discover how to build a support network of people who can provide you with encouragement, accountability, and feedback.)

Introduction:

Success rarely happens in isolation. Building a support network of people who can provide you with encouragement, accountability, and feedback is crucial to achieving your goals. In this chapter, we'll explore the benefits of having a support network and provide strategies for finding and cultivating relationships that help you succeed.

Benefits of Building a Support Network:

Having a support network has several benefits:

Encouragement: Your support network can provide you with the encouragement and motivation you need to keep going, especially during tough times.

Accountability: Your support network can hold you accountable for your actions and help keep you on track towards achieving your goals.

Feedback: Your support network can provide you with feedback and constructive criticism, helping you improve and grow.

Networking: Your support network can introduce you to new opportunities and help you expand your professional and personal network.

Strategies for Building a Support Network:

1. Identify your needs:

The first step in building a support network is identifying what type of support you need. Do you need someone to provide emotional support, help with specific tasks, or professional guidance? Understanding your needs can help you identify the right people to add to your network.

Story Example:

Daisy realized that she needed a mix of emotional support and professional guidance to help her achieve her goal of becoming a published author.

2. Reach out to people:

Don't be afraid to reach out to people who can help you achieve your goals. This could include mentors, coaches, colleagues, or even friends and family. Reach out to people who have experience in areas you need help with.

Story Example:

Daisy reached out to a published author in her genre who provided her with guidance and feedback on her writing.

3. Attend events:

Attending events related to your goals or interests is a great way to meet new people and expand your network. Look for conferences, workshops, or networking events in your area or online.

Story Example:

Daisy attended a writing conference where she met other aspiring writers and industry professionals who became part of her support network.

4. Participate in online communities:

Participating in online communities, such as forums or social media groups, is a great way to connect with like-minded individuals who share your goals or interests.

Story Example:

Daisy joined a Facebook group for writers where she connected with other aspiring authors and received feedback on her writing.

5. Give back:

Building a support network is a two-way street. Don't just focus on what you can get from others, but also on what you can give back. Providing support, feedback, and encouragement to others can strengthen your relationships and help you build a more robust network.

Story Example:

Daisy provided feedback and encouragement to other aspiring writers in her writing group, which helped her build stronger relationships and expand her network.

Conclusion:

Building a support network is essential for achieving your goals and succeeding in life. By identifying your needs, reaching out to people, attending events, participating in online communities, and giving back, you can build a strong and supportive network that helps you grow and thrive. Remember, success is rarely achieved alone, and having the right people by your side can make all the difference.

10. Managing Stress:

Strategies for Coping with Stress and Avoiding Burnout

(This chapter teaches you how to manage stress and avoid burnout, so you can stay focused and energized as you work towards your goals.)

Introduction:

Stress is an inevitable part of life, but when left unchecked, it can lead to burnout and negatively impact your health, productivity, and overall well-being. In this chapter, we'll explore strategies for managing stress and avoiding burnout, so you can stay focused and energized as you work towards your goals.

Understanding Stress:

Stress is the body's response to perceived threats or challenges. It can be caused by a variety of factors, including work, relationships, finances, and health issues. While stress can be a motivator, chronic stress can lead to burnout and negatively impact your physical and mental health.

Signs of Burnout:

Burnout is a state of emotional, physical, and mental exhaustion caused by chronic stress. Signs of burnout include:

- Feeling tired and drained most of the time

- Decreased productivity and effectiveness

- Withdrawal from responsibilities and social activities

· Increased cynicism and negativity

· Physical symptoms such as headaches, muscle tension, and stomach problems

Strategies for Managing Stress:
Here are some strategies for managing stress and avoiding burnout:

1. Identify Your Stress Triggers: Identify the situations and events that trigger stress for you. Once you know your stress triggers, you can develop strategies to manage or avoid them.

Story Example:
Daisy identified that her stress triggers were tight deadlines, conflicts with coworkers, and financial worries.

1. Practice Self-Care: Make time for self-care activities such as exercise, meditation, and spending time with loved ones. Self-care helps you recharge and reduces the negative effects of stress.

Story Example:
Daisy practiced self-care by going for a run after work, meditating for 10 minutes in the morning, and spending time with her partner and friends on weekends.

1. Set Boundaries: Learn to say no to commitments that aren't essential or that cause excessive stress. Set realistic expectations for yourself and others, and communicate your boundaries clearly.

Story Example:
Daisy set boundaries by declining invitations to social events that interfered with her writing schedule and communicating her workload and availability with her coworkers.

1. Practice Mindfulness: Mindfulness is the practice of being present and aware of your thoughts, feelings, and surroundings. Mindfulness can help reduce stress and increase your resilience to stressful situations.

Story Example:

Daisy practiced mindfulness by taking short breaks throughout the day to focus on her breath and surroundings, and using a mindfulness app to meditate during lunch breaks.

1. Seek Support: Don't be afraid to seek support from friends, family, or mental health professionals. Having a support system can help you manage stress and avoid burnout.

Story Example:

Daisy sought support from a therapist when she was feeling overwhelmed with work and personal stressors. She also leaned on her partner and close friends for emotional support.

Conclusion:

Managing stress is essential for maintaining your physical and mental health and achieving your goals. By identifying your stress triggers, practicing self-care, setting boundaries, practicing mindfulness, and seeking support, you can effectively manage stress and avoid burnout. Remember, taking care of yourself is not selfish; it's necessary for achieving success in all areas of your life.

11. Overcoming Perfectionism:

How to Let Go of Perfectionism and Embrace Imperfection

(Here, you'll learn how to overcome perfectionism and embrace imperfection, so you can make progress towards your goals without getting stuck in self-doubt or fear of failure.)

INTRODUCTION:

Perfectionism can be a double-edged sword. While striving for excellence and doing your best can lead to success, perfectionism can also lead to stress, self-doubt, and a fear of failure. In this chapter, we'll explore the negative impact of perfectionism and provide strategies for overcoming it, so you can make progress towards your goals with confidence and self-acceptance.

The Negative Impact of Perfectionism:

Perfectionism is a mindset characterized by an intense desire to be flawless in all aspects of life. While striving for excellence can be a good thing, perfectionism can be harmful and have negative effects on your mental and physical health, including:

· Stress and anxiety: Perfectionists are often worried about making mistakes and may feel overwhelmed by their high standards, leading to chronic stress and anxiety.

· Procrastination: The fear of not being perfect can cause perfectionists to delay taking action or making decisions.

· Self-doubt: Perfectionists may constantly doubt their abilities, even when they've achieved success.

· Fear of failure: The fear of not meeting their own impossibly high standards can make perfectionists avoid taking risks or trying new things.

· Burnout: Perfectionists may work excessively hard and neglect self-care, leading to burnout.

Strategies for Overcoming Perfectionism:

1. Set Realistic Standards: Accept that perfection is impossible and set realistic standards that align with your values and goals. Focus on progress rather than perfection.

Story Example:
Daisy realized that her obsession with perfectionism was causing her to procrastinate and feel stressed. She decided to set more realistic standards for herself, such as writing for an hour a day, rather than trying to write the perfect novel in one sitting.

1. Challenge Negative Self-Talk: Recognize and challenge negative self-talk that reinforces the belief that you must be perfect to be successful. Replace negative self-talk with positive affirmations.

Story Example:
Daisy realized that her inner critic was constantly telling her she wasn't good enough. She challenged this negative self-talk by reminding herself that

she was making progress towards her goal and celebrating small wins along the way.

1. Embrace Failure: Failure is a natural part of the learning process. Embrace failure as an opportunity to learn and grow, rather than a reflection of your worth.

Story Example:

Daisy used to fear failure and would avoid taking risks in her writing. She realized that failure is a natural part of the creative process and started to view rejection as an opportunity to learn and improve her writing.

1. Practice Self-Care: Take care of your physical, emotional, and mental health. Prioritize self-care activities that help you relax, recharge, and stay balanced.

Story Example:

Daisy used to neglect self-care in favor of writing. She realized that taking breaks, practicing mindfulness, and engaging in physical activity helped her feel more energized and productive in her writing.

1. Seek Support: Build a support network of friends, family, or a therapist who can provide encouragement, feedback, and perspective.

Story Example:

Daisy found that sharing her struggles with writing and perfectionism with a supportive writing group helped her feel less alone and more motivated to keep writing.

Conclusion:

Perfectionism can be a significant barrier to achieving your goals. By setting realistic standards, challenging negative self-talk, embracing failure, practicing self-care, and seeking support, you can overcome perfectionism and make progress towards your goals with self-acceptance and confidence. Remember, progress, not perfection, is the key to success.

12. Mindset Mastery:

Developing a Positive Mindset for Success

(This chapter explores the power of mindset and teaches you how to develop a positive mindset that supports your goals and helps you overcome challenges.)

Introduction:

The power of mindset cannot be overstated when it comes to achieving success. Your mindset is the lens through which you view the world and the beliefs that shape your thoughts, feelings, and actions. In this chapter, we'll explore the concept of mindset and how it affects your success. We'll also provide strategies for developing a positive mindset that supports your goals and helps you overcome challenges.

The Importance of Mindset:

Your mindset has a significant impact on your success. Research has shown that people with a positive mindset tend to be more resilient, motivated, and successful than those with a negative mindset. Here are some ways that your mindset can affect your success:

Beliefs: Your beliefs shape your thoughts, feelings, and actions. If you believe that you can achieve your goals, you're more likely to take actions that support your success.

Resilience: A positive mindset can help you bounce back from setbacks and challenges. It allows you to see challenges as opportunities for growth and learning rather than as failures.

Motivation: A positive mindset can increase your motivation and drive. When you believe that you can achieve your goals, you're more likely to put in the effort required to make them a reality.

Strategies for Developing a Positive Mindset:

Developing a positive mindset is not a one-time event but a continual process of self-reflection and growth. Here are some strategies that can help you develop a positive mindset:

1. Practice Gratitude:

Gratitude is a powerful tool for developing a positive mindset. It allows you to focus on what you have rather than what you lack and can help you shift your perspective towards the positive. Take a few minutes each day to reflect on the things that you're grateful for.

Story Example:

Daisy started a gratitude journal where she wrote down three things she was grateful for each day. This simple habit helped her focus on the positive aspects of her life and develop a more positive mindset.

2. Challenge Negative Thoughts:

Negative thoughts can sabotage your success and lead to a negative mindset. When you catch yourself thinking negatively, challenge those thoughts with evidence to the contrary. Ask yourself if your thoughts are realistic or if you're catastrophizing.

Story Example:

Daisy struggled with negative thoughts about her writing ability. Whenever she caught herself thinking negatively, she challenged those thoughts by reminding herself of positive feedback she had received from readers and her own accomplishments.

3. Focus on Growth:

A growth mindset focuses on learning and growth rather than fixed abilities and traits. Embrace the idea that your abilities can be developed through hard work and dedication. View challenges as opportunities for growth and learning rather than as failures.

Story Example:

Daisy adopted a growth mindset when it came to her writing. She viewed each rejection as an opportunity to learn and improve her craft rather than as a personal failure.

4. Surround Yourself with Positive People:

Your environment plays a significant role in shaping your mindset. Surround yourself with positive people who support your goals and encourage you to grow and develop.

Story Example:

Daisy joined a writing group where she connected with other writers who shared her passion for writing. Being around like-minded individuals who shared her goals and encouraged her to pursue them helped her develop a more positive mindset.

Conclusion:

Developing a positive mindset is essential for achieving success. By practicing gratitude, challenging negative thoughts, focusing on growth, and surrounding yourself with positive people, you can develop a mindset that supports your goals and helps you overcome challenges. Remember that developing a positive mindset is a continual process that requires self-reflection, dedication, and a commitment to growth and development.

13. Celebrating Your Wins:

How to Acknowledge and Celebrate Your Accomplishments Along the Way

(Here, you'll learn why it's important to celebrate your wins and how to acknowledge your accomplishments
along the way.)

Daisy had always been a hard worker. She set high goals for herself and worked tirelessly to achieve them. But she also struggled with acknowledging her own accomplishments. She was quick to move onto the next task without taking a moment to appreciate what she had achieved. This left her feeling unfulfilled and burnt out.

One day, Daisy's friend suggested that she start celebrating her wins, no matter how small they may seem. At first, Daisy was hesitant. She didn't want to seem boastful or arrogant. But her friend explained that celebrating your accomplishments doesn't have to be about bragging or showing off. It's about acknowledging the hard work and effort that went into achieving them.

Daisy decided to give it a try. She started by creating a list of all the goals she had accomplished in the past year, no matter how small they seemed. She included things like finishing a challenging project at work, learning a new skill, and taking care of her mental and physical health.

As she looked at the list, Daisy realized that she had accomplished a lot more than she had given herself credit for. She started to feel a sense of pride and satisfaction in her achievements.

From then on, Daisy made a point to celebrate her wins. She would take a moment to reflect on what she had accomplished and how it had helped her move closer to her larger goals. She would treat herself to something special, like a nice meal or a relaxing day off. She also started sharing her wins with her friends and family, who were always happy to celebrate with her.

Daisy found that celebrating her wins had a profound impact on her mindset. It helped her feel more confident in her abilities and more motivated to keep working towards her goals. She also found that acknowledging her accomplishments helped her avoid burnout. By taking the time to celebrate her wins, she was able to recharge and come back to her work feeling refreshed and energized.

If you struggle with acknowledging your accomplishments, know that you're not alone. Many people find it difficult to celebrate their wins, especially if they are perfectionists or have impossibly high standards for themselves. But taking the time to acknowledge your accomplishments, no matter how small they may seem, is crucial for your mental health and wellbeing.

Here are a few tips for celebrating your wins:

1. Keep a list of your accomplishments: Write down every goal you achieve, no matter how small it may seem. Keeping track of your accomplishments can help you see how much progress you've made over time.

1. Reflect on your achievements: Take some time to reflect on what you've accomplished and why it's important to you. Think about how it has helped you move closer to your larger goals.

1. Treat yourself: Celebrate your wins by treating yourself to something special. It doesn't have to be anything big or expensive, just something that makes you feel good.

1. Share your wins with others: Don't be afraid to share your accomplishments with others. Your friends and family will likely be happy to celebrate with you.

Remember, celebrating your wins is not about being boastful or showing off. It's about acknowledging your hard work and effort, and taking the time to appreciate what you've accomplished. By celebrating your wins, you'll feel more motivated, more confident, and more energized to keep working towards your goals.

14. Adapting to Change:

How to Navigate Change and Keep Moving Forward

(In this chapter, you'll learn how to adapt to change and stay flexible as you work towards your goals.)

Introduction:
Change is a natural part of life, and it's essential to learn how to adapt to it. As Daisy pursued her goals, she faced unexpected changes that required her to be flexible and adaptable. In this chapter, we'll explore how to navigate change and stay focused on your goals despite unexpected obstacles.

The Importance of Adapting to Change:
Adapting to change is critical for success because it helps you:

1. Stay Resilient: Adapting to change helps you bounce back from setbacks and remain resilient in the face of adversity.
2. Stay Focused: When you're adaptable, you can stay focused on your goals despite unexpected obstacles.
3. Stay Relevant: Adapting to change allows you to stay relevant and up-to-date in a rapidly changing world.

Navigating Change:
Here are some strategies to help you navigate change:

1. Accept Change: The first step in navigating change is to accept it. Change is inevitable, and it's essential to embrace it rather

than resist it.

2. Stay Positive: A positive attitude can help you navigate change more effectively. Focus on the opportunities that change presents, rather than the challenges.

3. Be Flexible: Being flexible allows you to adapt to change more easily. Be open to new ideas and ways of doing things.

4. Seek Support: A support network can help you navigate change and provide you with encouragement and feedback.

5. Embrace Learning: Change often requires learning new skills and knowledge. Embrace learning as an opportunity for growth.

6. Set New Goals: Change may require you to adjust your goals. Take the time to reassess your goals and make any necessary adjustments.

Story Example:

Daisy faced unexpected changes when her publisher went out of business, leaving her without a way to promote and sell her book. Daisy had to adapt quickly to this change and find new ways to reach her audience.

Adapting to Change:

1. Accept Change: Daisy accepted the change and acknowledged that it was outside of her control.

2. Stay Positive: Daisy stayed positive and looked for new opportunities to promote her book.

3. Be Flexible: Daisy was flexible and explored new marketing strategies, such as social media and book clubs.

4. Seek Support: Daisy reached out to her support network of fellow writers and readers for advice and encouragement.

5. Embrace Learning: Daisy embraced the opportunity to learn about new marketing strategies and how to engage with her audience in new ways.

6. Set New Goals: Daisy adjusted her goals and focused on

building a stronger online presence and growing her email list.

Conclusion:

Adapting to change is essential for success. By accepting change, staying positive, being flexible, seeking support, embracing learning, and setting new goals, you can navigate unexpected obstacles and keep moving forward towards your goals. Remember, change is inevitable, but it's how you respond to it that makes all the difference.

15. Maintaining Momentum:

How to Stay Focused and Motivated for the Long Haul

(This chapter teaches you how to maintain momentum and stay focused and motivated over the long term, so you can achieve your life goals and live the life you want.)

Introduction:

Achieving long-term goals requires sustained effort and consistent action. However, it can be challenging to maintain momentum and stay motivated over the long haul. In this chapter, we'll explore strategies for maintaining momentum and staying focused on your goals, using the story of Daisy as an example.

Story Example:

Daisy had been working on her goal of becoming a published author for several years. She had written and self-published several novels and had gained a small following of readers. However, she still felt like she had a long way to go to achieve her ultimate goal of becoming a best-selling author and earning a living from her writing.

Daisy knew that maintaining momentum was critical to achieving her long-term goals. She had experienced periods of low motivation and burnout in the past, and she didn't want to fall into that trap again. So, she set out to develop strategies for staying focused and motivated for the long haul.

Strategies for Maintaining Momentum:

Here are some strategies that Daisy used to maintain momentum and stay focused on her goals:

1. Celebrate Your Wins: Celebrating your wins, no matter how small, can help you stay motivated and focused. Take time to acknowledge and appreciate your progress towards your goals.

Story Example:

Every time Daisy finished a novel, she would take a day to celebrate her accomplishment. She would go out for a nice dinner or treat herself to a spa day. This celebration helped her stay motivated to continue writing and working towards her long-term goals.

1. Stay Accountable: Accountability can be a powerful motivator. Find someone who can hold you accountable for making progress towards your goals.

Story Example:

Daisy joined a writing group where members would share their writing goals and hold each other accountable for making progress towards those goals. This group helped Daisy stay focused and motivated to keep writing.

1. Create a Routine: Creating a routine can help you stay on track and make consistent progress towards your goals.

Story Example:

Daisy created a writing routine that included writing for one hour every morning before starting her day job. This routine helped her make consistent progress towards her writing goals, even on days when she wasn't feeling particularly motivated.

1. Set Milestones: Setting milestones can help you break down larger goals into smaller, more manageable tasks. This can make

it easier to stay motivated and focused.

Story Example:

Daisy set milestones for each novel she wrote. For example, she would set a milestone to finish the first draft, then the second draft, and so on. This helped her stay focused and motivated throughout the writing process.

1. Take Breaks: Taking breaks can help you avoid burnout and stay energized over the long term.

Story Example:

Daisy would take breaks from writing to do other things she enjoyed, like hiking or attending a concert. These breaks helped her recharge and stay motivated to continue writing.

Conclusion:

Maintaining momentum and staying focused on your goals is critical to achieving long-term success. By celebrating your wins, staying accountable, creating a routine, setting milestones, and taking breaks, you can maintain momentum and stay motivated over the long haul. Just like Daisy, you can achieve your long-term goals and live the life you want.

About the Author

Dilbagh Singh, a passionate individual from Delhi, India, who believes that everyone has the potential to turn their dreams into reality. Dilbagh is a graduate of Delhi University and has spent years researching and exploring different strategies to help individuals achieve their life goals. With his book, "From Dream to Done: Strategies for Achieving Your Life Goals," Dilbagh shares his knowledge and expertise to help readers overcome obstacles, stay motivated, and reach their full potential. This book is a culmination of Dilbagh's years of experience and is a must-read for anyone looking to turn their dreams into reality.

www.ingramcontent.com/pod-product-compliance
Lightning Source LLC
Chambersburg PA
CBHW061630130726
47996CB00003B/1199